THE TEACHING BOOK

*The Age of the Lily,
the High Time After the Time:
God in Us,
and We in God*

The Age of the Lily,
the High Time after the Time:
God in Us, and We in God

*The eternal word,
the one God, the Free Spirit,
speaks through Gabriele,
as through all the prophets of God –
Abraham, Job, Moses, Elijah, Isaiah,
Jesus of Nazareth,
the Christ of God*

THE TEACHING BOOK

*The Age of the Lily,
the High Time
after the Time:
God in Us,
and We in God*

Gabriele
Publishing House

The Teaching Book
the Age of the Lily
the High Time after the Time
God in Us, and We in God

1st Edition June 2021
© Gabriele-Verlag Das Wort GmbH
Max-Braun-Str. 2, 97828 Marktheidenfeld, Germany
www.gabriele-verlag.com
www.gabriele-publishing-house.com

Original German Title:
Das Lehrbuch
Das Lilienzeitalter,
die hohe Zeit nach der Zeit:
Gott in uns und wir in Gott

The German edition is the work of reference for all questions regarding the meaning of the contents.

Translation authorized by:
Gabriele-Verlag Das Wort GmbH

All Rights Reserved.

Order No. S 187en
ISBN: 978-3-96446-192-6

Printed by: KlarDruck GmbH, Marktheidenfeld, Germany

Contents

The time, it will most surely come 7

The path into the Age of the Lily:
God in us, and we in God 9

Everything is energy –
Everything has consciousness 12

Every one determines their self each day –
We are called upon 15

In the Age of the Lily, at the beginning of
the New Era, we set the course for our
day already in the morning 20

The beginning of the Age of the Lily –
to become free of ourselves for the New Era:
God in us, and we in God 25

We are surrounded by God, who is the All-life –
True life is prayer 30

The day – an unimaginable book for insight 34

The true life is the eternal life 41

*Let us clear out the all-too-human in us,
in order to again find our true nature:
spirit of His Spirit* 46

*The blood, our mirror image.
The human being at the low point
of degeneration* 50

*We ourselves are called upon, for
the transformation of each one* 60

*Every life's expression is registered –
Our film reels are active, day after day* 64

*We are asked how we want to deal
with the All-Life* 69

The time, it will most surely come …

The time, it will most surely come, before the world goes under, there will arise a kingdom of peace and unity. A place of noble, free men, and free from themselves, too. A covenant of true ones, unto the Spirit true.

It shall not be a temple to which the people go; and thus, there be the same mark on all there to be seen. And where just one should remain, he won't be overcome. It is the power of love which will over all prevail.

God, in His love will gather from all around this Earth, a band of faithful fighters and form the covenant. No heart can then resist Him and joyfully submits to the One who then rules as King, the New Jerusalem.

The people now have risen and shall be led by Him, to whom alone all honor and thankfulness is due. It has so long been written and is in God's great plan, what by this people is in His will now being done.

(Text C. Hilty 1833 and Universal Life)

The path into the Age of the Lily: God in us, and we in God

The Age of the Lily is at the beginning of a New Era: Building New Jerusalem under the sign of love and love for neighbor, in God, the Father-Mother-Being, the All-law of love. The love for God and neighbor is the primordial-eternal law of heaven, which is omnipresent.

God is love. God's love is the strongest power; it is the All-power in infinity. God, the love, the All-law of love, flows throughout all suns, all planets, all Being.

Of course, the material cosmos with the planet Earth is also part of this – everything that is on, in and above the Earth bears the life, the breath of God, the love, the law of the All.

The beginning of the Age of the Lily is already showing the way to the eternal love. In few words, the path is called:

God in us, and we in God.

The Age of the Lily, the beginning into the New Era, bears the messianic name of the Co-Regent of the Eternal Kingdom, of the Son of God, once in Jesus of Nazareth, His instructions for the Kingdom of Peace of the Christ of God, the word of the Christ of God, once in Jesus of Nazareth:

But the Comforter, the Holy Spirit, whom the Father will send in my name, he will teach you all things and bring to your remembrance all that I have said to you.

When the Spirit of truth comes, he will guide you into all the truth, for he will not speak on his own authority, but whatever he hears he will speak, and he will declare to you the things that are to come.

The Wisdom in God, in the Christ of God, has come to the people to teach them what it means: God in us, and we in God.

We go into the New Era, step by step.
Thereby, we do not disregard the symbol of the lily.

The lily, the purity of life, goes with us step by step into the primordial eternal law of the love for God and neighbor.

God's love is the All-power, the love of neighbor. God's love is the life in the soul of the ensouled human being. In every cell of our physical body, in every blood vessel, in all the components of our body, is the life, God.

The soul of the human being and all the components of the physical body are set in the word "life," which means that everything has consciousness and, ultimately, the corresponding state of consciousness, according to the maturity, that is, the degree of maturity of the soul and of the human being.

Everything is energy –
Everything has consciousness

Everything is based on energy. Since everything is energy, everything also has its corresponding degree of maturity and present state of consciousness.

No matter what name we people give to the life on Earth – everything has consciousness, from which the further state of consciousness develops. The further development or unfoldment of consciousness is also called evolution or growth or maturity.

As mentioned: Everything is energy – and is based on sending and receiving. Energy has forms, colors, fragrances and sounds. Energy cannot be destroyed, only changed. But everything is permeated by the primordial eternal law, which is God's unfailing love.

Because everything is based on the energy of differing consciousness, it can be said that: The different degrees of consciousness are in constant communication, on the one hand, with the same energetic degree of consciousness, and on the other hand, with all the already developed states of consciousness.

Every developed state of consciousness sends and receives, yet in everything is life's core of consciousness, which is solely in communication with the All-life, the All-law, God, which is the love.

Wherever we human beings go and are, and even when we use vehicles or other means of transportation – the human body remains connected to the Earth.

Everything is consciousness. Whether we look up or down, to the right or to the left, everything has consciousness, because everything bears the All-life, the eternal All-law of the Being, God.

Once we human beings become aware of this, we also understand that there is nothing that is dead, because consciousness is life and communication.

As stated, there is nothing that is dead. What we term unpalatable or even dead has parts that communicate and therefore, transforms. The substance that develops from this is still active life, merely in a different form and with the corresponding degree of consciousness.

People have various outlooks on life and on what life means. Seldom do we people think about what life actually means. Everything that disintegrates, that is no longer usable by us people and is cleared away, regardless of what objects they may be, bears consciousness, which contains in itself the transformation.

The four elements fire, water, earth and air are also consciousness.

Everything is energy. Our food, as well, our drinks, the clothing, furniture and more are consciousness. The state of consciousness is completely different, but everything is based on energy. The human being, too, is one single body of energy. Every function of our body, every organ, all glands, hormones, bones, tendons, ligaments, blood vessels etc., etc., have different degrees of consciousness and depend on each other.

As stated: Every body is an energy body of different frequency, that is, vibration, and every vibration rate is consciousness. Every person has his specific state of consciousness, which requires the appropriate food or medicine, yet, everything is based on energy, on the respective state of consciousness.

Every one determines their self each day – We are called upon

When it comes to personal predispositions and inclinations, it is usually said: "We have brought our predispositions with us, perhaps from our parents, grandparents or from a relative in the more distant past."

This can be possible – let us consider that the people of the so-called chain of ancestors walked the Earth before us and probably passed on their behavior patterns to their descendants and the descendants, in turn, to their descendants. But regardless of what genetic material our ancestors passed on to us – we are called upon.

Our ancestors had their time, now, we have our time.

Even if we believe in reincarnation and think about who we might have been in the chain of ancestors, today, wc are asked what we are doing with our life, regardless of what we presume to have brought with us.

The word "life" could contain the solution to the riddle, because today and now we are called upon; every single one of us human beings is called upon – and not about how the other one does things.

No matter what we may have inherited or brought with us from our ancestors or where this or that may have come from – we are called upon, because we are the ones who are living now and today.

Thus, each one of us are asked how we have done and are doing with our life. This is decisive and can help us to resolve things from the past and to shape the future in a way that corresponds to the present existence that we term "our life."

The solution to the riddle can be deduced from the world of our feelings, sensations and thoughts that have been nourished until today, from our behavior toward ourselves and toward our fellow people, and also in relation to the animal and plant world.

Until we are fully aware that everything, but really everything, is based on energy, we should pause and reflect again and again, on the following statement: "Everything is based on energy."

As stated: The human being, the physical body, is an energy body, and is thus, energy.

We, every single one of us, determine ourselves each day. This means that we build up our physical energy through our daily behavior patterns, or we reduce our energy level, solely through our way of life, which is shown in our behavior patterns.

May it be repeated:

We determine each day the for and against – which means: an increase of energy or a decrease of energy – by our behavior patterns, which is the same as our way of life and which consists of our feelings, sensations, thoughts, words and actions.

Thus, we, every single one of us, are called upon.

Some people quite rightly say: "On the one hand, we get older every day; on the other hand, our nutrition is also important." That's true, but let's remember that everything is based on energy.

We ourselves weigh and measure what we eat and how much we consume. And we may very well be getting older from year to year, but here, the question is: "Am I getting old, or am I getting older?" Again, it's up to each one. Analyzed more precisely, this means: Do we get old through the years, or decades, or do we get older during this same time?

What I, Gabriele, want to express with this is that we, each one of us, determine it ourselves through our behavior patterns, which refer to the five components of life, that is, egoity components of feelings, sensations, thoughts, words and actions. We, that is, every single one of us, is called upon, and not the other one.

Therefore, the personal school of life for a life of the New Era in the Age of the Lily.

The path to the inner life, to the true life, goes into a more light-filled future.

Jesus of Nazareth taught us the eternal All-One God, the Father of love, whose Spirit is in the very basis of our soul, thus, God in us.

God, the eternal law, the life, the Spirit of truth, is in every ensouled human being and in every soul. The omnipresent Spirit is the All-life, He is the love and faithfulness to all His sons and daughters.

Nature, which likewise bears the All-life, can be a good teacher for us human beings, if, for example, we think of the seasons, of the becoming and the passing, in order, however, to again be in spring.

In the Age of the Lily, at the beginning of the New Era, we set the course for our day already in the morning

Dear fellow people, our day doesn't first begin after breakfast. Already upon awakening, it can convey something to us from the night, and already upon awakening, we begin to think.

The first thought in the morning is the personal thought of each individual, which comes from their world of programs. Here, too, an example from nature can be helpful. Many a plant species awakens in the morning to the next blossom.

Through our behavior patterns, each one of us determines their personal world, their life's programs. This is the corresponding barometer of our disposition, which is traced back to our five egoity components, to our feeling, sensing, thinking, speaking and acting.

As stated: We are called upon, not the other one. Therefore, we should get into the habit of not thinking or attributing our behavior patterns to other people.

Each one of us has a mind to measure and to weigh, no matter who wants to instill something in us or how we were brought up.

We are called upon – not in terms of what may have been yesterday, but of who we are today and what we make of it.

Back to our world of thoughts, which has something to tell us already on first awakening. It is our first thought. The first thought can already stimulate our disposition and attune our nervous system. And already then, we can find ourselves in the midst of one of our program situations. Therefore, right at the beginning of the day it is: We are called upon.

How do we decide? – because our disposition already wants to set the direction for the day.

No matter what lies before us, we are called upon: How do we want to go about it?

In the Age of the Lily, at the beginning of the New Era, we already set the course of our day in the morning. On the one hand, we weigh and measure our disposition and, on the other hand, our day's program. To weigh and measure means to analytically think over what concerns us.

In doing so, we monitor ourselves, our own world of thoughts.

As stated, the morning of our day already has a lot to tell us. While taking breakfast, for example, we learn: "Stop, not so hasty as before." Thus, we try to eat, drink and think more consciously. This means that we begin to change our thinking in terms of our hectic pace. Many a one thinks: "I'm in a hurry; I don't have time to eat consciously, to chew and drink consciously." Despite all this, what holds true is that only personal experience leads to mastery.

If you should accept the beginning of the day, endeavoring to calmly get ready for the day and take your breakfast consciously and quietly, you will soon notice that you hardly need more time for this than usual, quite the contrary. You will become or remain calmer, and the beginning of the day already has a completely different note.

The Age of the Lily leads to the New Era. The true prayer means to live consciously.

Should there be enough time, then we briefly stand at the window and look into the firmament. If we have little time, because the clock always determines our everyday life, then, when we are underway or when we go to our vehicle, we will briefly look at the firmament – an exercise that does not immediately bear fruit, but let us stay with it!

In time, we notice that each day may well have its own thoughts, but suddenly and unexpectedly thoughts rise up in us that until now were not so familiar to us. What does this want to tell us?

The message is that each day is your day, and that your day speaks to you. Already in the early morning, your day begins with the first thought.

At some point you have input the messages of the day yourself, either in your subconscious or in your soul, from where your day speaks up and brings you the message that you need to work on today. For those of us who strive toward the New Era, this means to live consciously.

The more you, that is, we, analytically think through our daily instructions – which does not mean that we do not carry out our daily work and the instructions of our supervisor – the more we will soon notice that we become calmer and are able to think and work more analytically.

We will carry out the work we have to do much more consciously and with more concentration. Without wanting to justify ourselves, we accept the matter, because that's just the way it is. In our everyday life, everything has advantages and disadvantages, but who is going to change that, if not us? We are called upon.

For each one of us the day is our day, and therefore, each one of us is also called upon.

Once we become aware of the fact that we are called upon in every situation, we begin to question ourselves more and more, in order to put our thoughts in order and perhaps to analyze our soliloquies. By doing this, we see behind many a loss of energy.

*The beginning of the Age of the Lily –
to become free of ourselves
for the New Era:
God in us, and we in God*

We are standing before a mighty time of radical change. A New Era is dawning and wants to give us an understanding of the Age of the Lily.

The Age of the Lily contains the teachings of the Christ of God, once in Jesus of Nazareth: "God in you, and you in God" – because in everything is the word of the All.

The word of the All is the word of the Creator-Spirit in all of nature; in the entire All, in infinity, the word of creation speaks, which we call God. Our atmosphere, which we often call the sky, can also be termed the All-dome, under which all earthly plant species, the entire world of animals on Earth, every stone and all the minerals have their place on Earth.

The four basic powers of God – Order, Will, Wisdom and Earnestness, on Earth called the four elements fire, water, earth and air – provide for the forms of life on Earth.

The Eternal Kingdom, the eternal Being, is the eternal homeland of all beings from His Spirit, as well as all forms of life.

The infinity, the Being, is communication.

In a divine revelation that helps us to recognize many things, we have already heard that evolution, that is, the communication of the forms of development, begins in the four planes of development, called the cradle of creation of the Being.

Dear fellow people, our change of thinking toward the true life has the goal of our becoming divine again, just as the true God taught us via Moses in the Ten Commandments and via His Son, the Christ of God, in His Sermon on the Mount.

Life means the All-life, which is beauty and purity. In this, the lily is an example for us. We learn, in order to find our way back to our true eternal life.

We begin to learn in what the occurrences of the day point out to us.

That is the beginning of the Age of the Lily, of the pure and balanced and of the free: to become free of ourselves for the New Era, for the Messianic, Sophianic Age, God in us, and we in God. With reference to the individual, this means: God in me, and I in God.

Under the sign of the Lily, of the New Era, we will gradually become free of ourselves, free of soliloquies, of prologues and monologues, free of unpleasant secrets.

If we continue to cultivate our soliloquies, prologues and monologues in an unchecked way, then, in time, these will enter our subconscious and then our soul as a program. In this way, we program ourselves.

The subconscious can become a not-inconsiderable bearer of secrets, which, from time to time, appears during the day and also at night before it becomes engraved in our soul, fixed in the soul particles, and at some point, is due to be cleared up or even comes into effect. Thus, our personal aspects can be very multifaceted, which, in many situations, want to tell us many a thing so that they can be worked off, for example, when sadness or arrogance or something far more serious comes over us.

Often, we seek help. Under the sign of the lily, of freedom and purity, we go to God in us, because we are the temple of God, and the true God is in us, therefore, God in us, and we in God.

There are many possibilities to withdraw in order to pray in us, to God in us. During our work for the day, there are also interruptions, for example, a pause in our work or after the noon meal, if there is still time, or on the way home, or at home. In time, we notice that prayer is life and the true life makes us free.

Prayer also means to look for the true life that we can perceive everywhere, be it in the firmament or in the raindrop that flows along the windowpane, for example, when we are just getting into our car. Whether we look into the firmament or pay attention to the raindrop on the windowpane – much, indeed, everything, wants to communicate with us, because the life is omnipresent.

Let us take note: The true God is the omnipresent Spirit of life.

The All, the infinity, is the *I Am the All-life*, and we are His children, His sons and His daughters. We should again become what is inherent in the core of being of our soul, the being of the Being.

That is why it is: become free of ourselves.

The lily is a symbol for this. It wants to remind us of our true nature, of the purity and beauty, of the cosmic life, which we are in the core of our soul.

We are surrounded by God,
who is the All-life –
True life is prayer

hus, prayer means to live according to the law of life.

Life is the All-unity, which the firmament, nature, the stone, each flower, each tree, each bush, each animal shows us. It is the word of the All.

Every ray of the sun that we notice can contain a message. Every breath of wind that moves our hair or caresses our face can hold a message for us.

Let us remember: God in us, and we in God.

The true God is the infinity.

It is the Father-Mother Being.

The eternal Being gave itself the spiritual-divine form, so that all His sons and daughters can behold Him, the primordial Being of the Being, which is active with them in the All-unity of the Eternal Kingdom.

Since the Eternal is also present as a Being among His sons and daughters, they also recognize their creations as the images of the Father-Mother-Being and, at the same time, they recognize that they are heirs of infinity.

All Being is consciousness and has the respective state of consciousness that is evolution in the Creator, in the Father-Mother-God, which means further development.

Ever more, and ever more deeply, we understand what prayer, in reality, means: to again become what the core of our soul bears, our true being.
To become that again is our task, which leads to the true life, to the sonship and daughtership in God, the Father-Mother-Being.
Therefore, every minute of our life on Earth is precious.

The life of infinity pulsates in the very basis of the soul of every ensouled human being. Life is so manifold and diverse that we human beings can never fully grasp the All-life in detail. But we experience and grasp ever so much more, if we begin to truly live, because, as stated:

True life is prayer,
God in you, and you in God.

The true Eternal God is the All-life. Life proceeds in sequences of consciousness, in immeasurable currents, in the mighty courses of eons.

Every ensouled human being has their spiritual state of consciousness, which they can bring to blossom, because wherever human beings go, wherever they are, they are surrounded by the true life and thus, by the true All-One God.

Whether we walk or drive to work, whether we do our work as a woman or mother – we are surrounded by God, who is the All-life.

Many a one asks: "Who or what is God? Who or what is the All-life?"
Whether we are familiar with the word "God" or with the concept of the "All-life," it is always the mighty All-one stream, the eternally flowing law, God, which we do not behold and which, nevertheless, surrounds us and flows through us. It is

the law of love, of the eternal Being, whose sons and daughters we are, whether we want to accept it or not.

Every single one of us human beings has their present state of consciousness, because every single one has burdened their soul – the one more, the other less. That is why we are called upon, every single one of us.

The day –
an unimaginable book for insight

The state of consciousness guides us according to our spiritual degree of maturity and purposefully calls our attention to something that would have something to say to us now and today.

Who calls a person's attention to their state of consciousness?

It is the all-flowing law, God, the Being, that flows through infinity, through every atom, every molecule, through all the suns and planets. God is the Being, the *I Am the primordiul eternal law eternally*, which – as stated – permeates infinity.

Nothing, absolutely nothing, is dead. There is nothing dead; everything has consciousness, which means life – even if this or that is ever so inconspicuous and seems pointless or useless to us human beings. No matter how we see it: Everything is subject to transformation, everything, even that, which we human beings declare as dead or even useless.

Therefore, for each one of us, the day can become an unimaginable book for insight and a corresponding reference book of immeasurable dimension.

As already explained: Today is indeed today, but the morning, the beginning of our day, is already preparing the message for those who awaken from their morning slumber. Each one is called upon, without ifs and buts. The message for the beginning of the day, as well as for the ongoing day, has been input by each one of us, at some point in time.

The morning and the day want to tell us – since it is a message for us – what is due to be recognized and cleared up and which often holds our thinking captive, blocking it.

What the day reveals can hold us as if captive, when the same thing keeps coming to mind again and again, because it wants to be remedied. When we become aware of this, we should – as far as it is possible – take a few minutes to ask ourselves what it has to say to us.

If we take seriously what ultimately concerns us, then our disposition may become somewhat uneasy, because our nervous system is trying to set things in motion that let us realize what needs to be done.

If we do this as far as we can, our disposition will soon become calmer and a great deal lighter.

Often it is our neighbor who can bring our disposition, our nerves, into turmoil. There are many occasions that upset us, yet, at the same time, hold a message for us. This or that or even our neighbor does not correspond to our present frame of mind.

Often it is merely a little thing that upsets our disposition. For example, something has been lying there the whole time where it does not belong. Disappointed and annoyed, we put it aside today and think: "Who put that there and didn't put it away? Why today of all days?" We continue to think: "Who was it? Why didn't they put it away? It could have been done long ago; it has been bothering me for a long time, and now, I'm the one that has to put it away," etc., etc.

Stop – the question: Did tidying up do me any harm? Or did it accomplish something on my path into the New Era?

I suddenly remember: It is necessary to become free of myself. This means: On the one hand, tidying up what someone else left behind helped me; on the other hand, I learned that how others do things is none of my concern. I simply put it away because it doesn't belong in this place, and that's the end of it.

Another vivid picture:
I go through the garden; suddenly I stumble over a small stone that always lies there and has its place there.
I look down and see there: In the border of the flowerbed a flower has opened, smiling at me with its color, as if it had a message for me. It does have a message: Stop and think about the All-life, and open yourself to the life.
The flower and also other things like grasses, perennials, shrubs, etc., remind us of the lily of purity and of the beginning of a New Era.

Or: Unexpectedly a word or a sentence comes up in you that stimulates a certain sense of freedom and joy.

This, too, is not by chance, just as everything in our existence is not a coincidence. Everything can tell us something.

Even a hint that delights us can be an impulse from nature, for example: Become free of yourself and of what others want and do, how they think and what they expect – unless you can help, then, when needed.

A day has many opportunities for self-recognition, so that we find ourselves and become free of ourselves. Especially the evening can become a time of rest, if we have recognized and remedied some things.

These are the first steps to true prayer. The true eternal God, who is the life in all things, does not need strenuous lip prayers. He, the All-love, wants us to begin to again live our heavenly heritage, to again love – which means: God in us, God in all things, for God is the life.

The true eternal God is the speaking God, the All-life.

The beginning of a change in our way of thinking means – spoken to each one of us:
Love the omnipresent life and eliminate the personal monologues, the soliloquies, which means: Become free of yourself.

Among other things, what are monologues?
On the one hand, it is talking to yourself; on the other, it is making an image of yourself or of others and running it through the mill of an imaginary world, until you are a part of it yourself, and, if possible, you become the main character.

This can go so far that the person believes themselves to be that person. From this, then follows the disparaging of one's neighbor, the know-it-allness and the outside influence and heteronomy, if we do not stop the whole "spell" of the ego in time.

Let it be repeated: Our task for a God-conscious humankind is to become free of ourselves.

I also call this becoming empty or being empty for the moments of the day, because a moment can already make us aware of many things and convey much to us.

Therefore, the motto is: Use the day; use the moment!

Only then, if we become free of ourselves, can we understand the life, the All-life, for the word of God is the All-life.

The true life is the eternal life

What is life?

In truth, there is only *one* life, even if every person speaks of their life.

To question ourselves, everyone would have to ask the question of themselves: What is "my" life, and how long does it last?

Quickly and without further thought, most of us would say: "Well, now, from birth to death." If we merely count the years, that's correct.

Even if we just say "the years from – to," many a one already begins to think. Is it decades or merely years, hours, minutes, seconds?

We cannot predict our time of life on Earth; nor can we measure and weigh it. We can only ask ourselves in the evening, at the end of the day: Did we make use of our day, also in regard to our attitude toward life?

Were we living or often merely vegetating? Were we preoccupied with ourselves a lot, for example, in prologues and monologues?

The questions to ourselves could also relate to the past. Every evening the question could be:

"Have I lived? How often was I concerned with myself, and what does that mean in view of my life's energy?"

Dear fellow people, we are coming closer to ourselves!

Where were we with our thoughts, when we drove to work or walked our old familiar path?

We know the mighty tree at the wayside, or the shrub that's now blooming again, as it does every year at the same time.

We know when something blooms in our garden, or when here or there in the garden a flower or other growing plants need water, or the name of the flower that is blossoming again today at the same time on the window sill, etc., etc.

When it rains, we see the drops of water that beat on the window panes during a heavy rain etc., etc.

Yes, we live!

The question is: Is this truly our life, or is it the preschool to life, or did we just briefly pass by on this planet, or is it enough for us to be a human being?

I hope that many of us people think about this.

A few more questions to get to the point of the schooling for life:

Why are there so many kinds of flowers, large and small? Why so many different kinds of shrubs, bushes and trees? When we look at the foliage or compare one flower with another from the same tree or shrub, we notice that none is the same as the other.

And if we take the trouble to compare one stone with another of the same kind, we notice that no two stones are alike, nor are the "veins" that run through the stone, etc., etc. The bark of a tree, too, is indeed like the bark of another tree of the same kind, yet structured differently.

On the whole, one could ask questions ad infinitum.

We human beings cannot fully and completely grasp and fathom the diversity of life – and yet, in all Being is the speaking God.

From the origin of all Being, the life speaks to us:
I Am the life, the All-law of infinity and the Infinite.
My child, let yourself be guided; best of all, let yourself be guided by Me, the I Am, because you are omnipresent life from Me, the I Am – I Am the life!

Dear fellow people, we practice, we learn, because before us lies the way into the New Era, which announces eternity.

In us, in the very basis of our soul, the eternal, the true life, wants to make itself felt. Wherever we go, wherever we are – everything is based on communication.

Jesus of Nazareth taught us human beings that we are the temple of God, and that God, the true life, dwells in us.

The primordial word of His All-presence comes from the innermost part of our soul, from the core of being, and gives life to the soul and to the physical body. Likewise, the whole cosmos is permeated with the eternal, true life. The speaking God is omnipresent life.

The true life is the eternal life, which manifests itself in the *I Am the I Am, the law, eternally.*

I Am the I Am is the primordial eternal law, eternally. It flows from the Sanctum of the eternal Being and is active in all of infinity.

As stated: It is the eternal life. It also flows in the very basis of our soul and communicates in every component of our existence.

As already stated, the very basis of our soul is the core of being, which is in communication with the Infinite, the *I Am the I Am, the All-law, the life.*

It flows into our body and wants to reveal to us that in the very basis of our soul, we are a being of eternity, the being of the Being, the essence of the Kingdom of God.

*Let us clear out the all-too-human
in us, in order to again find
our true nature:
spirit of His Spirit*

We are called upon, every one of us – to change our way of thinking:

We have literally buried our body cells, the functions of our body, all the components of our body, under the rubbish of our ego – the one more, the other less.

That is why we can hardly perceive anymore, or even not at all, the Being, God in us, the Father-Mother-God, the life.

Jesus of Nazareth spoke in the following sense: *You are the temple of God and God dwells in you.*

We want to let this come true in us by beginning to clear away the rubble of the all-too-human aspects in us, and find "God in us" again, His omnipresent love, which is the eternal life. Just as the life, the I Am, the law, eternally flows through infinity, so does it fill the nature kingdoms with life – everything is communication.

Every stone, every plant species, every animal is in the consciousness of communication with the *I Am the I Am, the primordial, eternal law.*

And how is it with us human beings?
Communication simply means sending and receiving.

It cannot be repeated often enough:
The almighty All-Sender is in us and gives our body the strength to exist.

To what extent we are willing to take in the transmitting potential of the Being depends on us.
Do we continue to cover it up each day through our egomania, which has innumerable components, that is, facets, or do we uncover it, by gradually working through the "rubble" of our base ego, in order to receive the All-sender, the life?
Well, we are called upon!
The primordial eternal life is always present. We receive according to our state of consciousness.

Every ensouled person receives, because every soul has the receiver in itself.

As stated: All of infinity sends, because everything lives and transmits. We perceive it according to our state of consciousness.

Everything, absolutely everything, is permeated by the eternal Spirit, God. All Being receives according to its state of consciousness and emits its present state of consciousness.

The New Era is coming toward the willing people.

Therefore, the motto is: We learn to again find our eternal homeland, the eternal Being, in ourselves, in the very basis of our soul, by affirming ourselves as a being in Him, in God.

The eternal law streams through infinity. It is His word, eternally.

The divine beings live and communicate in this consciousness. They are in the All-stream of communication, beings from His Spirit – spirit beings.

Our path leads back again, in order to merge into the word, which is the All-communication: *I Am the I Am, the primordial eternal law.*

May it be repeated:

Our true being is spirit of His Spirit, the word, the I Am, which is communication.

We learn what communication means: First of all, we try to receive; secondly, we learn to send.

We human beings do indeed send out our presence on a daily basis, but in our all-too-human sending potential, the question of what we want to hear in response, that is, receive, is usually pending.

The New Era has grand plans.

We begin with the nature kingdoms. Later it continues with the animal world and then somewhat higher with the rays of the planets.

What was merely briefly indicated is not a game.

Hence the indication: In the basis of our soul we are spirit beings.

What the term "spirit beings" wants to tell us is: to be spirit of His Spirit, beings of His Spirit.

The blood, our mirror image.
The human being at the low point
of degeneration

When we consider that in the eternal Being everything is in communication with everything, then we gradually grasp how pathetic humankind has become. People depend on technology to communicate with other people here and there. Humankind is striving to expand ever more on technology.

And so-called science is looking for further knowledge, whereby it usually fishes in murky waters, on matter.

An example: The human being is still a long way from thinking about what blood is all about and what blood contains.

The cell consciousness and the blood, the blood flow, were created by the wrong behavior of former spirit beings, which increasingly led to degeneration, because the ethereal current became more and more dense.

The process of becoming human can be ascribed to the gradual condensation, also called thickening, of former spirit beings.

As long as people wage wars, kill animals, slaughter animals and consume their flesh, blood is shed.
Have we human beings ever thought about why the blood stops flowing when a person no longer breathes? We accept everything just as it seems. Breathing is crucial. It simply requires oxygen and nitrogen, elements that we also call air and that are important for our breathing.

People think just as little about the demise of the material body. "All logical," they say – "It is simply logical that the body withers and decomposes when it has passed away."
Of course, it starts to decay and then soon starts to smell – so, is it all logical?
Why is it different in nature?
The tree falls, the shrub withers, the flower wilts and nature gives up its annual output in autumn. In nature, withering or passing away has nothing

to do with death, because in spring, when the time is right, it gives its flowering life back to the Earth.

Nature as a whole does not have to be buried or burned right away because you cannot stand the smell of the remains anymore.

The animal is similar to the human being; the animal also has blood.

May the following be food for thought:
The blood carries substances that are a hindrance for transformation, that is, for the All-communication.

The animal is mostly inaccessible to people due to the behavior patterns of human beings, through the deprivation of freedom, animal transports, hunting, factory farming, and the killing and consumption of meat.

As already stated, I call the egoity components feeling, sensing, thinking, speaking and acting. These five egoity components affect our five sensory components: seeing, hearing, smelling, tasting and touching.

I compare blood with a mirror, in which each of us can see ourselves as a mirror image. The mirror image does not correspond to our neighbor, that is, to the other person. We are the ones.

It is our correspondences that are an obstacle to the communication with the All-law of life.

The technology of humankind is also in opposition to the eternal law of communication.

We human beings are ultimately against everything that we cannot see and grasp. We are like dry wood in dirty waters. The human being as such is a degeneracy through the Fall.

As already reported in many divine revelations, the Fall, the density, is nothing but transformed-down light ether, that is, energy that became coarse-material through the Fall-experts, who wanted to see things differently than the Eternal, whom we human beings call God.

When one considers that everything is based on energy and everything flows together into unity, which is the Eternal and that emanates from the Eternal, and that people's communication network exists solely through technology, then one senses what kind of image we human beings provide.

As revealed by the Cherub, the Prince of the eternal Wisdom: utter degeneration – in its darkest form.

The human beings as such are a consumer bundle of energy, in order to maintain themselves.

In many divine revelations, we read about ensouled people and about not-ensouled people.

Jesus of Nazareth said: *The Kingdom of God is within, in you.* The one who does not possess what is "within," the soul with the core of being, is merely a mass, that is, a person without a soul.

The ensouled person does indeed have a soul, whose core of being is the essence of the Kingdom of God, which the Christ of God protected with the Redeemer-spark, His divine heritage.

By taking back the spiritual loan to the Fall-experts, coarse-materiality is also gradually dissolving, for infinity is and remains eternally fine-material.

According to iron laws, all that is not ensouled is gradually being led to the earth in order to be transformed according to law and order.

Let us return to the beginning of our topic: God in us, and we in God.

How can people liberate themselves from the concept of being the crown of creation, which allows itself everything – against so-called second-class people, against animals and nature?

Solely by changing their thinking and, not lastly, by turning away from their prayer formulas to a "god," who only demands and directs humankind according to his arbitrary law, which compels, but does not give.

The coercion of faith is like a drug that forces people to do what religion dictates.

In the times of times, this led to the inner impoverishment of the people and ultimately, to the abuse of the life of nature and of the animal world, because the transformed-down human body needed more and more food, all the way to the consumption of the flesh of its fellow creatures.

The All-communication is the way for people to turn back in the coming time, in the New Age that is announced.
For people of the New Era this means that we are called upon to gain freedom by breaking away from the dictatorship of idols.
At some point, every one of us human beings will ask themselves how they kept the Ten Commandments of God and the Sermon on the Mount of Jesus, the Christ?
Did we pay attention to our egoity components of feeling, sensing, thinking, speaking and acting, in order to question these and transform them? And what about the five sensory components, seeing, hearing, smelling, tasting and touching?

The questions to ourselves can go further:
With what did I feed my blood, and via my blood, with what did I nourish my nerves, organs

background, then where the slide sits is more about flow. Focus on telling a good story that is complemented by your team slide rather than the other way around.

Articulating the points covered above allows founders to justify the components of a business model to themselves before investing further into an idea. During the writing of your plan/deck, you may identify risks that compel you to change the business model or even the industry focus.

Now, **a couple more tips** before moving on to the next section:

- Avoid putting a valuation on your deck/plan (unless you are finalizing a round). Investors may ask for this figure in person, but you are likely to prevent future dialogue if you put the valuation on paper and it is either too big or too small for the investor. By omitting it, the investor focuses on what matters: what you are trying to build.
- The second tip is that a cap table (which we will cover shortly), is a handy thing to include in your plan/deck . (Though, perhaps you won't have space for it when you are presenting in person). A cap table is useful mainly for subsequent discussions, but can greatly help an investor understand everyone's motivations. I always recommend you build your own cap table, although these days there are plenty of online resources to help you.

Remember, one of the best things you and your team members can do very early on is draft a pitch deck/plan, no matter how simple, that you feel can represent your company and communicate the value of your opportunity without requiring your physical presence to pitch it.

A note on platforms, and as previously mentioned, I've seen most companies now using DocSend or similar document distribution platforms to distribute their decks to investors so that they can:

1. Update their deck 'live' without having to re-send the deck via email. This makes updating mistakes and other things much easier.
2. Allows you to track who views the deck (if you choose to collect emails) and other interesting metrics about how it is viewed.
3. Makes distribution faster as 'size' of download is irrelevant, making it easier to share over messaging apps like WhatsApp/Telegram etc.

In addition to DocSend, I'm increasingly seeing people make use of publishing tools such as Notion pages with some of their key attributes to share with investors, in effect, replacing the Deck altogether with a more dynamic structure. Feel free to experiment with what works for you and the type of investors you are courting.

Your Financial Assumptions Model

In addition to the above materials, you will likely be asked for a quantification of your cash milestone assumptions to see how you think through your costs and revenue-generating activities.

The reason why I call this the "financial assumptions model" is because calling it a financial "plan" this early in your company's development is misleading. As we've covered in the Milestones section, very rarely do your projections for Day 63 or Day 105 truly happen. Standing at Day 1 (or before), you can't know what the future holds. So, think of the financial assumptions model as a representation of how your cash needs are affected by your growth assumptions.

Later in this book, we cover how an investor reviews your financial plan, but for now, start thinking about how to present your company's expenses and revenue expectations and how they affect your cash burn in an easily readable spreadsheet.

For some templates to jog your thinking about how to visually present the financial models, search for "Christoph Janz SAAS Dashboard" as a starting point, and check out the Visible.VC's financial modeling page; it has some great materials, including deck templates. Check out additional resources at the end of the book.

Your Pitch

By now, I hope it has been impressed on you that storytelling is a key part of the fundraising process. The human mind was designed to process stories as a way of recalling important information regarding meaningful things from the past. Refining your verbal storytelling artistry is a worthwhile investment, as it will help you channel your pitch more effectively.

When thinking about your company, think about the underlying story behind it. Why are you doing this? Why you? Why your team? And perhaps most importantly, "Why Now?" As some VCs might say, it is the only non-negotiable (e.g. Don Val) — "Why Now" was the only question Jensen Huang of Nvidia could answer at seed!

There are many ways to tell stories. While pitching for

fundraising will have many elements of traditional storytelling, it isn't entirely about dramatics. Storytelling is also about efficiency. Some startups are tempted to us certain storytelling clichés such as "the long build-up with a surprise ending" but when it comes to fundraising, you're better off keeping your technique simple.

Specifically, you should be able to quickly explain what it is you do, why you do it, for whom (your customer), and why now. In the next chapter, we will cover storytelling in more depth.

Deal with your Elephant

Almost all pitches have an elephant in the room, something about your company that will consume the mind of the listener until it is addressed. You will lose people if you go too far into your pitch without addressing your Elephant.

Examples of Elephants include a competitor of yours that just raised money or just died or a company that's just like yours. Don't hide from your Elephant—address the issue upfront and comprehensively. That way, you'll build more trust and conviction that your opportunity is the right one.

I cover getting your Elephant under control more in this book's Appendix.

Your Cap Table

One quick way an investor can get a feel for how founders see each other's roles within an organization is by reviewing a company's equity distribution for each shareholder. This is called your cap table.

In order to read some of the terms on a cap table model, below are some definitions you might find useful:

In reality, human beings are an interweaving of bluster and affectation, with the aim of being right. They continue to build up this milieu until they are repugnant to themselves. Then they gradually begin to see reason and try to find themselves.

Where can one begin?

As stated – with the five egoity components: What do I think I'm feeling? What do I sense; what do I think and what am I saying? What do I want to touch and what do I touch?

All five components together are illusions, which may very well have a lot of content, but which can be explored, only when people really want to change their way of thinking and not only according to appearances.

We ourselves are called upon, for the transformation of each one

The fact that we are not *only* a simulacrum, that is, an illusion, can also be deduced from our five sensory components, when a balance, a proportion, in our general habits and eating habits is established. This means a certain refinement of the physical aspects toward the spiritual.

> If we notice that in ourselves, then we feel:
> Now, the real, deep schooling, begins:
> God in me, and I in God.
> The divine is the omnipresent –
> the omnipresence is God.

Our egoity components point the way, because each day is our day. Every one of us lives their day. Especially sight and hearing often point the way. Where am I looking? What do I see? What do I feel or think thereby? Among other things, this would be a hint to ourselves. It is really worthwhile to pause, for example, when we are driving, to look briefly for a parking possibility, in order to perhaps note down what the eye or the ear has told us and then, when we have a little more time, to question ourselves.

Or when we are underway on foot or otherwise occupied: Let us write down what our eyes and ears tell us.

If we are given the possibility to do so, let us question ourselves as to whether our feelings or thoughts were consistent or whether we were merely content with the shells of our feelings and thoughts, etc., etc.

Even if this were so, our feelings and thoughts nevertheless have content, because everything is energy. Everything that we feel and think, all our ten components – the five egoity components and our five sensory components – have content, even if we think that something was merely spoken or thought "mindlessly."

The body of every human being consists of its ten components. Even if we speak of the body as such, which we take for granted – everything is based on our specific contents. Every component of our body, down to the last fiber, has content, whether we want to accept this or not.

Dear fellow people, ultimately, as human beings, each and every one of us is a unique illusion, a system without equal. Seen in this light, one can say: We speak of ourselves, but we do not know ourselves.

Despite everything: The time it will most surely come, before the world goes under, there will arise a kingdom of peace and unity. …

In the end, the solution lies in the transformation of each one. That is why, again and again the statement: We are called upon.

If we consider that the true eternal God is the omnipresent Eternal One, then we may also assume that the true eternal God is also in us, in the very basis of our soul. In order to approach the very basis, the core of being of our soul, we should change ourselves to the effect that we, as people with souls, become aware that the true eternal God is the speaking God.

Therefore: Wherever we look, wherever we go – everywhere is God, the Creator-Spirit, the speaking All-consciousness.

Whether we look at the firmament and let it reverberate in us or look more closely at a tree, a bush, a flower or a stone – we will soon feel that a deep resonance begins to vibrate in us, which, however, we should not force.

*Every life's expression
is registered – Our film reels are
active, day after day*

As already reported: Each day is the personal day of each individual. We should pay attention to our five egoity components and question them, depending on what the day reflects to us. So, we are called upon.

Everything is based on energy. Our often so casual afterthoughts and phrases in passing, our uncontrolled speaking and also our actions could be compared to film reels on which we record everything, including what runs "just on the side."

In every situation we are called upon, and not the other one, even though we may think the other one is partly to blame.

It may well be that this is the case, but we are called upon to see what is pending with us. Everything, but absolutely everything that concerns us, that comes from our egoity components, we record, for example, on our film reel or even reels.

Our film reels, which record us as image and sound, are active day after day – it is we ourselves – and show us how much we can remedy each day.

If we make use of our days to remedy the ungood, we will soon notice that we start the day, that is, tackle it, more relaxed and easily, because we are increasingly finding the way to ourselves, and are thus analyzing more joyfully what moves us just "by chance."

As stated: There are very many things that the day wants to point out to us. It is always our system; it is always our inputs, our systematic film reel principles.

Our day wants to make us aware of many things. For example: A blade of grass pokes up between two stones. Unnoticed by many people who use the stony path and despite our old familiar way of thinking, it makes us aware that it, too, is a part of life.

We have learned to pause for a moment, if time and the surroundings allow. Our sense of sight triggered a great deal in the consciousness of our world of feelings and thoughts.

We notice that many, often very many, memories or thoughts or previous conversations come in-between. We look closer, but our thoughts have already carried us further – already, we are totally somewhere else.

This is the reel, indeed, these are the reels that have recorded our life on Earth thus far.

In all honesty: In reality, we don't know who we are, yet everything is recorded and retained on the corresponding reels. That is why it is important to find ourselves, in order to reach our true nature again, and be with God, the Eternal All-One, who is active in the very basis of our soul.

This means moderation and discipline.

Dear fellow brothers and sisters, it is worthwhile to find oneself, for example, in what all we have recorded on our reels. Soon we will realize that on many a reel we always find the same habits and even abnormalities. Once we have worked through some things, we notice that the other reels also become thinner. On the one hand, because we often recognize and tackle the same habits of thinking and speaking with always the same content, on the other hand, with lightness and open-mindedness. We become more and more attentive to ourselves, that is, more alert regarding our day, which – as stated – has a lot to say and point out to us.

We increasingly find our way to ourselves. Our advisor is a specialist; it is our day.
Soon we will also be aware that already in the morning we have arrived at our day.

So let us give ourselves a chance to experience ourselves by reorienting our ten components.
Thereby, we will not only become calmer – we will gradually perceive ourselves in a completely different way. We will be able to analyze what was absolutely necessary before, and figure out what is necessary today.

The all-too-human concern is also part of this, to have to communicate at all costs and, if possible, in conversation with a mode of expression that ensures that we are the center of attention.
What do we get out of this?

We discover thereby that we lack energy, which someone else should give us.

We learn: We try to take ourselves back in the same or similar situations. The analysis of ourselves already points out to us what we notice about ourselves. We begin to change ourselves more and more toward the positive.

With self-analysis, we experience on ourselves that we are calmer and more stable in ourselves. The change is a refinement of our nature.

Through this, we also learn to look at everything more closely. Building on this foundation means not to make ourselves dependent on people and religions.

*We are asked how we
want to deal with the All-life*

God, the Eternal, gave us the Ten Commandments through Moses and the Sermon on the Mount through His Son, the Christ of God.

When we recognize our offences, which can come from the soul or from our subconscious, then we compare these with the Ten Commandments of God and the Sermon on the Mount. From this, we see our further path – God in us, and we in God.

The heavenly Father-Mother-God knows about all His children. He, the Almighty, has beheld in Himself all of us, every single one of His children, and, from Himself, created us in His image, heavenly beings of the Being, which we should become again.

An indication for us: to think again and again of the being in us.

In every movement, too, in all of infinity, is God, the All-law of the eternal Being.

The Father-Mother-God, the Creator of infinity, is love.

When we become more light-filled in our thoughts, in our entire behavior, then we will often realize that a flower by the wayside is smiling at us or an animal is looking trustingly at us. We have received – God in us.

Again and again, we are asked, about how we want to act in the future, of course, with ourselves. Our life on Earth could be very fulfilled, if we recognize ourselves as a part of the whole, without expanding our ego, without wanting to be something.

If we make use of our day to draw closer to God in us, then we are surrounded by life, which is in us as essence and in the core of being of our soul.

We are asked how we want to deal with the All-life.

Solely we ourselves are called upon, because we, every ensouled human being, are the temple of

God, and the All-light, the All-love, is in us, in the very basis of our soul. The All-love is the Creator of all Being. It is the Father-Mother-God, who beheld us as His sons and daughters and created us in His image, spirit beings of His Spirit, God.

That is the beginning of the Age of the Lily for the New Era, God in us, and we in God.

We can also think – and, of course, relate to ourselves, personally: God in me, and I in God, the Father-Mother-Being.

Thus, we are called upon, every single one of us.

May I extend to you a spiritual lily on your lily-path?

Your sister in the spirit of love,
Gabriele